ITALY

A TRUE BOOK

by

**Christine Petersen and
David Petersen**

Children's Press®

A Division of Scholastic Inc.

New York Toronto London Auckland Sydney
Mexico City New Delhi Hong Kong
Danbury, Connecticut

An Italian girl
in school

Reading Consultant
Linda Cornwell
*Coordinator of School Quality
and Professional Improvement
Indiana State Teachers
Association*

Library of Congress Cataloging-in-Publication Data

Petersen, Christine, 1965–
   Italy / by Christine Petersen and David Petersen.
      p. cm. — (A true book)
   Includes bibliographical references and index.
   ISBN 0-516-22256-2 (lib. bdg.)   0-516-27360-4 (pbk.)
    1. Italy—Juvenile literature. [1. Italy.] I. Petersen, David, 1946– II. Title.
III. Series.
DG417.P48 2001
945—dc21   00-064384

Contents

A Rich and Rugged Land

Italy is a country in southern Europe. It is about twice the size of the state of Florida. Most of Italy is a peninsula—a narrow strip of land surrounded on three sides by water. On a map, Italy looks like a high-heeled boot.

The Leaning Tower of Pisa, one of Italy's best-known buildings. Nobody planned for this bell tower to lean.

In the north, Italy is capped by some of the world's most famous mountains, the Alps. Bordering Italy along the Alps

The Italian Alps

are the countries of France, Switzerland, and Austria. Slovenia lies to the northeast. The Apennines, Italy's second major mountain range, run like a zipper down the length of the "boot."

The Italian mainland extends 702 miles (1,130 kilometers) from the Alps to Cape Spartivento. South of Spartivento sits Sicily, the largest of many islands in the

Mediterranean Sea. Farther southwest, across the narrow Strait of Sicily, lies Italy's nearest African neighbor, Tunisia.

If you sailed along Italy's winding coast, you would pass through four different seas. North of the Ionian Sea—at the heel of the "boot"—lies the Adriatic Sea. On the west are Italy's two largest islands, Sicily and Sardinia. They mark the

An Italian couple and their baby enjoy a day at the beach.

border between the Tyrrhenian and Mediterranean seas.

Most of Italy is made up of rolling hills and mountains.

Here farmers grow various fruits on terraced hillsides. Italy's most important agricultural area is the Po Valley,

These people are having a good time harvesting grapes.

Valleys like this one, south of the Alps, produce plentiful crops.

south of the Alps. This fertile
valley produces plentiful
crops of grains, vegetables,
and grapes. Wheat is grown
in southern Italy, along with

olives and citrus fruits. Wheat
is used to make the dough
for spaghetti and other kinds
of pasta.

A chef makes spaghetti in the
kitchen of his restaurant.

Early Italians

Italy's earliest recorded civilization dates back about 3,200 years. The Etruscans were clever engineers who built roads, bridges, and irrigation canals to water their crops. Etruscan craftspeople made beautiful pottery, jewelry, and metalwork. Etruscan scholars

invented number and alphabet systems, and warriors built a powerful army.

The Etruscans made beautiful gold jewelry (left). This clay block with Etruscan writing is about 2,400 years old (below).

After eight hundred years of power, the Etruscans began to lose battles for their lands. The city of Rome—now the capital of Italy—won its independence from the Etruscans about 2,500 years ago. Rome was soon at the center of a powerful military empire.

The "golden age" of ancient Rome began in 31 B.C., during the rule of Emperor Caesar Augustus. Within a century, Rome's powerful armies had

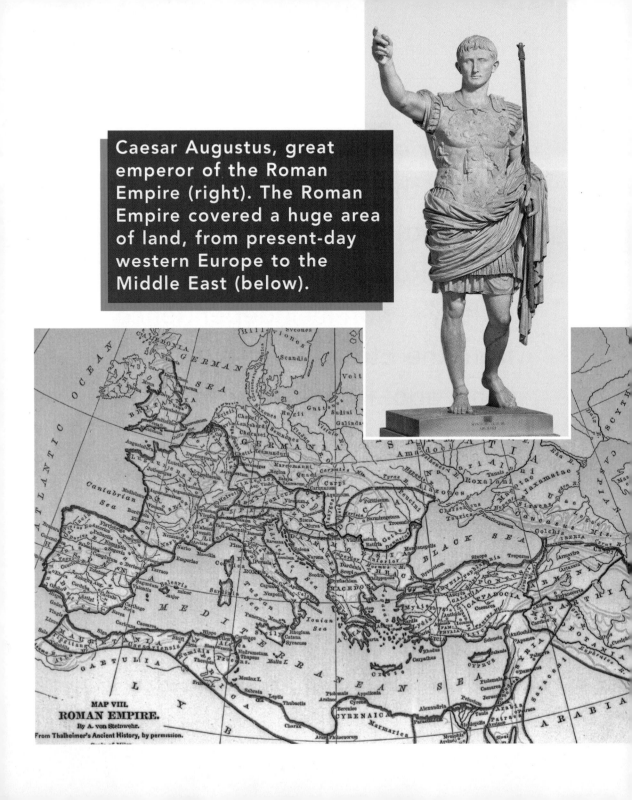

Caesar Augustus, great emperor of the Roman Empire (right). The Roman Empire covered a huge area of land, from present-day western Europe to the Middle East (below).

conquered a vast area from Great Britain to Asia.

Ancient Rome, like modern Rome, was a crowded and busy place. Poor people lived in cramped apartments, while wealthy Romans enjoyed great luxury. Their homes were filled with lovely statues and paintings, and slaves did all the work.

In ancient Rome, only children from wealthy families attended school. Boys studied math and writing, and they practiced making speeches like their fathers. Girls were taught to run the household. Poor children were schooled at home—if at all—and they had to work to help support the family.

After five hundred years, the Roman Empire finally ended. In A.D. 476, Emperor Romulus Augustulus surrendered to the barbarian king Odoacer.

Romulus Augustulus, the last Roman emperor, surrenders the empire to Odoacer in A.D. 476.

Volcanic Disaster

Italy is a country that rocks and rolls. Small earthquakes, powered by some of Europe's largest volcanoes, make the ground shake and tremble almost every day.

One morning in A.D. 79, as people in the seaport towns of Pompeii and Herculaneum went about their business, a volcano called Mount Vesuvius erupted suddenly. There was no time to escape as hot ash rained down, burying towns, houses, people, and animals.

As Mount Vesuvius sprays smoke and fire, people in Pompeii scramble for safety.

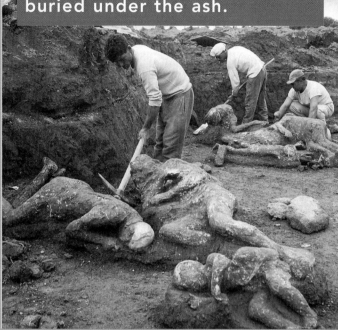

When Pompeii was excavated, these bodies were found buried under the ash.

Recently, Pompeii and Herculaneum were carefully excavated, or uncovered. Now visitors can walk around the lovely buildings that were once centers of social life—bath houses, gyms, temples, and theaters. These well-preserved ruins tell us how people looked and lived in the Roman Empire.

Even today, mighty Vesuvius belches smoke—a reminder that disaster could strike again.

The last eruption of Vesuvius happened in March 1944. The volcano still sends up smoke today.

The Birth of a Nation

While the ancient Roman Empire is long dead, the modern Republic of Italy is still a youngster. After the fall of Rome, the Italian peninsula was divided into many small kingdoms. In 1870, they were finally reunited under one king. In 1946, Italy became a

Members of the Italian parliament make the country's laws.

republic, governed by a president, a prime minister, and a parliament.

Today, Italy is a colorful blend of ancient and modern.

People look small next to the huge cathedral in Milan's town square.

Centuries-old cathedrals stand at the center of most towns. Stick-straight ancient Roman roads shoot across the countryside. The lovely cobblestone streets, built for

horses and carriages, are too narrow for cars. The streets are often filled with people, some walking and some riding bicycles or motorbikes. Towering above these reminders of an

This modern building combines old and new styles of architecture.

ancient past are modern skyscrapers. Speeding trains and jet planes connect Italy with the rest of the world.

A Floating City

"Water taxis" line up at the dock.

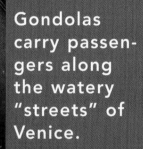

Gondolas carry passengers along the watery "streets" of Venice.

Like many Italian cities, Venice is filled with lovely old buildings. There is something very special about Venice, however—it's a "floating city." Instead of streets, Venice has canals. People get around in boats—"water taxis" called gondolas. The boatmen, or gondoliers, often sing to their passengers while pushing their boats along with poles.

Spectators cheer for their favorite gondoliers in a boat race.

The Mother Church

Rome, Italy's capital city, is the home of Roman Catholicism, one of the world's most important religions. There are about one billion Roman Catholics in the world.

In Italy, about 95 percent of the people are Catholic. The church is involved in weddings,

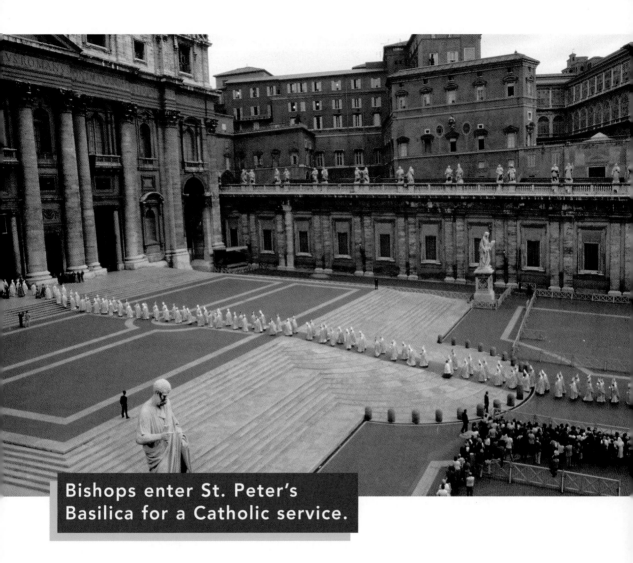

Bishops enter St. Peter's Basilica for a Catholic service.

funerals, and other important events in people's lives. On religious holidays, called *feste,*

Fireworks explode at a religious festival.

Catholic saints are honored with special foods, parades, and fireworks.

Vatican City is a tiny independent country inside the city

This girl holds a model of the baby Jesus. She and her friends are waiting for the pope to arrive.

of Rome. As the world capital of Catholicism, Vatican City is home to the most important person in the Catholic Church:

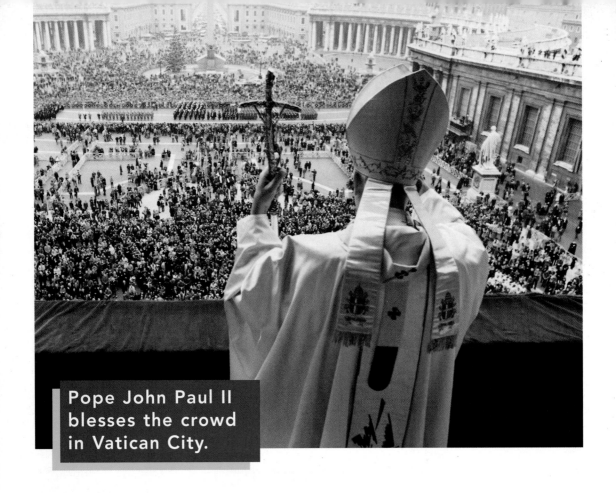

Pope John Paul II blesses the crowd in Vatican City.

the pope. Many people come to Vatican City to worship. Others come to admire the city's world-famous architecture, statues, and paintings.

Opera!

O pera is an Italian passion. An opera is a play performed live in front of an audience. Operas usually have large orchestras, fancy costumes, and beautiful stage sets. What really makes them special, though, is that the actors sing their lines. Opera was first performed in Venice in 1600. Today, opera singers, such as Luciano Pavarotti, are as famous in Italy as rock stars are in America. Almost every town has its own opera house.

Luciano Pavarotti, an Italian opera star, sings his lines with a powerful voice.

The Good Life

Italians are known for making the best of life, and the family is at the center of it all. Often, three generations—grandparents, parents, and children—live together. A family dinner in Italy is like a party, lasting up to two or three hours, with lots of

An Italian family

conversation, laughter, and
even singing.

Sports are an important
part of the good life in Italy.

A young athlete is ready for a game on the beach.

Most Italians enjoy soccer, tennis, and winter sports. They also love racing—cars, bicycles, dogs, horses, *anything*. Every

Italians will race just about anything that moves—including these horses at the Palio Festival in Siena.

year Italy spends billions of *lire* (Italian money) on sports, including support for the nation's Olympic teams.

A boy poses for his school picture in Sicily.

Education helps make Italy a successful modern nation. Free schooling is provided to children between the ages of six and fourteen. Students may attend trade and technical schools, art and music academies, or junior colleges called *liceo*. Italy also has many fine universities.

Today, Italy is recognized as the international center of the fashion industry. In cities such as Milan and Florence, clothing designers make works of art for people to wear.

Like any country, Italy has its problems, too. With 57 million people crowding the cities, good jobs are getting harder to find. Overcrowding also leads to air and water pollution, a rise in crime, and other serious problems.

Italy's people are working hard to solve their problems, however. The future of this country just might be even grander than its past.

Italy's people are working together for a bright future.

To Find Out More

Here are some additional resources to help you learn more about the nation of Italy:

Books

Arnold, Helen. **Italy.** Raintree Steck-Vaughn, 2000.

Haskins, Jim. **Count Your Way Through Italy.** Carolrhoda Books, 1990.

Hewitt, Sally. **The Romans.** Children's Press, 1996.

Simpson, Judith. **Ancient Rome.** Time-Life Books, 1997.

Organizations and Online Sites

The National Geographic Society
http://www.national geographic.com/

Use the Map Machine to find atlas information, physical and political maps, and satellite images of Italy.

The Etruscans
http://www.agmen.com/ etruscans/

Take a virtual tour of this ancient Italian civilization. Includes Etruscan history, art, and cities.

BBC's The Romans
http://www.bbc.co.uk/ education/romans/

A wonderful look at all aspects of life, art, and politics in ancient Rome. Includes a quiz to test your knowledge after reading.

Voyage Back in Time: Ancient Greece and Rome
http://www.richmond.edu/ ~ed344/webunits/ greecerome/

A colorful look at ancient Rome and Greece.

Important Words

citrus fruits acidic fruits, including oranges, limes, lemons, and grapefruit

civilization a highly organized society

empire a large land area ruled by an emperor

excavate to carefully dig up and search a piece of land

irrigation the process of supplying water to crops, often through ditches or canals

parliament a group of elected officials who make a nation's laws

pollution damage to air, water, or soil caused by people

prime minister the leader of a parliament

scholar a serious student; one who loves learning

terraced stepped on different levels, like stairs

Index

Meet the Authors

Christine Petersen grew up near the Pacific Ocean in California. She now lives in the lake country near Minneapolis, Minnesota. Christine is a biologist, educator, and expert on North American bats. She enjoys hiking, snowshoeing, reading, travel, and playing with her two cats.

David Petersen is Christine's father. David lives in a self-built cabin in the San Juan Mountains of Colorado. He has been writing True Books for more than twenty years, and knows that nature is life's greatest gift.